Jerry Linsom

BROKEN BONES BUT NOT A BROKEN SOUL

Jerry Linsom, Jr

Broken Bones But Not A Broken Soul

By: Jerry Linsom

Jerry Linsom

Copyright © 2022 by Trient Press

All rights reserved. No part of this publication may be reproduced, distributed, or transmitted in any form or by any means, including photocopying, recording, or other electronic or mechanical methods, without the prior written permission of the publisher, except in the case of brief quotations embodied in critical reviews and certain other noncommercial uses permitted by copyright law. For permission requests, write to the publisher, addressed "Attention: Permissions Coordinator," at the address below.

Criminal copyright infringement, including infringement without monetary gain, is investigated by the FBIand is punishable by up to five years in federal prison and a fine of $250,000.

Except for the original story material written by the author, all songs, song titles, and lyrics mentioned in the novel The Silent Wars are the exclusive property of the respective artists, songwriters, and copyright holder.

Trient Press

3375 S Rainbow Blvd #81710, SMB 13135

Las Vegas,NV 89180
Ordering Information:

Quantity sales. Special discounts are available on quantity purchases by corporations,associations, and others. For details, contact the publisher at the address above.

Orders by U.S. trade bookstores and wholesalers. Please contact Trient Press:

Tel: (775) 996-3844; or visit www.trientpress.com.

Printed in the United States of America Publisher's Cataloging-in-Publication data
Linsom, Jerry
A title of a book : Broken Bones Not A Broken Soul

ISBN

Hard Cover	978-1-955198-39-4
E-Book	978-1-955198-40-0
Paperback	978-1-955198-44-8

Broken Bones But Not A Broken Soul

Contents

CHAPTER 1	A Tale of Two Mothers
CHAPTER 2	Buttle Meets Pedestal
CHAPTER 3	Finding Identity
CHAPTER 4	A Tale of Two Accidents
CHAPTER 5	Recipe for Joy
CHAPTER 6	Spirituality and Slipping
CHAPTER 7	Getting the High out of High School
CHAPTER 8	Second Chance
CHAPTER 9	A Second Life
CHAPTER 10	Shifting Environment
CHAPTER 11	The Darker Side of Responsibility
CHAPTER 12	A Tale of Two Police Encounters
CHAPTER 13	Fast Food and Chicken Wings
CHAPTER 14	Deacon Jerry
CHAPTER 15	Hints of a Gift
CHAPTER 16	Deacon Jerry, Part 2
CHAPTER 17	Girl Problems

CHAPTER 18	Freeing Limitations
CHAPTER 19	Limiting Freedoms
CHAPTER 20	Serious Consequences
CHAPTER 21	Zero Comfort
CHAPTER 22	Zero Support
CHAPTER 23	Welcome to My Love Life
CHAPTER 24	Here Comes the Money
CHAPTER 25	Movement and Constants
CHAPTER 26	A Period of Farewells
CHAPTER 27	Death Lingers
CHAPTER 28	A Fresh Start
CHAPTER 29	Grief and Joy
CHAPTER 30	Love Completes Life
Connect With Me	
About The Author	

A Tale of Two Mothers

Chapter One

How much of what you are today is the product of your upbringing? If we go by the general trend of the ultra-wealthy families retaining most of their wealth while the newly rich ones losing their wealth within three generations, we can easily assume that there is some connection between one's upbringing and what they become later in life.

I am therefore blessed to have been abandoned. Let me rephrase that: I am fortunate to have been raised by my great aunt instead of my mother. My mother was easily overwhelmed by the prospect of raising me. I don't even blame or resent her for that. If she had gone ahead and raised me, I would have too many doubts about myself because she had doubts about me. But who wouldn't? I was born bearing signs that I wasn't going to be "normal."

The chief among them was my lazy eye. While many toddlers develop a lazy eye by the time they start walking, looking at a baby bearing that slightly cross-eyed look can be scary, especially if the child is your own. That's because such an unfocused gaze is often associated with mental illness. Long story short, my mother thought I would be mentally impaired and got overwhelmed by the idea of raising a child with special needs. And that's where my great aunt Nancy came into the picture.

The problem with my mom was that she assumed I was going to have special needs, and the issue I had with Nancy was that he gave me special treatment. I have plenty of gratitude towards Aunt Nancy because of the values she instilled in me and the discipline I got from her upbringing early on. These are essential to success in life.

But you know what else is essential? Falling down. If your persistence never gets tested, your potential never becomes visible. And that's what aunt Nancy unintentionally hindered. She put me in a bubble of sorts, and to this day, I don't know how to ride a bike because I was never allowed to try. In life, you fall, and you get up. And my childhood was where I never had the opportunity to get up. At least not by design.

However, despite my guardian's best efforts, chaos found its way to me. I discuss further how two physical accidents impacted me in a different part of this book. But I wanted to start off my story by briefly discussing what was different about me.

Sure, my physical condition is different, but the one thing that truly made the most difference was the chance in upbringing. I stayed with my mom on weekends at different periods of my life. I saw her get beaten by her boyfriend and asked myself, "why does she put up with this?" But had I grown up with her, I may have never asked that question. I could have built the opinion that "this is normal, and that's how you treat a partner." Instead, I learned to stand up for myself by observing Aunt Nancy. She was stern. She was loyal.

Twenty-eight years working at the same company: General Electrics. And while she worked there, she also managed to check in with my other brother (whom she also had guardianship of) at his school while accompanying me in the hospital where I used to be most of the time. I learned to overcome obstacles by seeing it was possible. And for that, one couldn't have a better example than my great aunt Nancy.

Buttle Meets Pedestal

Chapter Two

My brother and I got vastly different treatment, and it wasn't fair to either of us. But then again, life's not fair. He was always put on a pedestal where he was supposed to live up to the family's hopes and dreams. It was like being Lebron James Junior: everyone expects a degree of greatness from you. And while it is nice to have heads turn like that, it isn't nice to live up to that pressure.

But of course, as a child, I only saw the positives of being in his position. As they say, the grass is greener on the other side. And he was on a pedestal; I was in a bubble. I don't know if he saw my situation as envious because I did get a lot of attention and first-hand care. But I know I was sick of it.

If we were "riding" a bike, I was just sitting in the wagon while he was the one actually riding the bike. That picture is the best example of the pedestal and the bubble. The pedestal comes with an expectation of effort: he had to pedal and keep the bike moving, but it also isn't great to just be in the wagon with no option to drive yourself.

As a child, I did not have the sense to understand his position. This became even more complicated because he, too, was a child as he was younger than me. This made it impossible for either of us to see our respective conditions with adult sobriety. All I saw was him going to a more expensive school with classmates richer than us.

I, on the other hand, was left to attend a "ghetto" school. The kind of school where parents roll the dice sending their kids. Aunt Nancy didn't roll the dice, though. She had a history of helping schools, and she thoroughly believed that kids could get educated enough to have a chance in life despite attending one of these low-budget schools.

But going by the racial demographics and the truths of the time, you could see that the expensive schools had a majority Caucasian pupil-count while the "ghetto schools" were made up entirely of African Americans and occasionally other minorities.

On the surface, it seemed like a divide of color. A layer further was the divide in income. The school I went to was cheaper to go to. But above all, it was a divide of circles. My brother had his friends, and I had mine. And that is where the difference was the most evident. My circle was all black, and his school was mostly white. I don't care about what race either of our friends belonged to, but that visual difference at such a young age really cemented the fact that we were living in separate worlds.

Because of this, it was pretty hard for us to connect with each other. However, when our aunt passed away, we started to get closer. It is then that I discovered how our initial distance was all about prioritizing her approval and attention over each other. We were no longer competing to be her favorite or live up to her expectations. We were in the same boat: missing a great woman we owed a lot to.

Finding Identity

Chapter Three

I've briefly touched upon my school experience: I went to an all-black school initially and had to eventually get re-integrated into a racially mixed education system. People today do not understand that the racial divide didn't switch off over-night. The people who were segregated in any context were also the people who lived through desegregation.

Whether this desegregation happens within the same institution or is experienced as you move from one spot to a mixed spot, it is bizarre, to say the least. Let's explore what wasn't bizarre about my experience: finding my identity. For many black students, being in an all-black school gives them a common identifier to bond around.

Unfortunately, this wasn't the case with me. Sure, I was in a school where I was just like those around me in one aspect, but in their eyes, I was different in other ways. I knew this. They knew this. And that is where my early school experience became about fitting in.

Think back on your first day at school; you know how scary it is thinking about all the ways in which you might get picked on. As humans, we are extremely social, and we have a primal fear of being rejected by our "tribe."

Remember that for our ancestors, getting ostracized meant dying. That means most of our ancestors, dating back to the first men, were all careful about socially fitting in. It is in our genes. Now imagine how amplified that need is in a child who already knows he is different. And that's where I developed my class clown tendencies.

If I figured out ways to make them laugh with me, they wouldn't laugh at me. And among the hundreds of ways I discovered to make my classmates laugh, I knew the one way I didn't want to make them laugh: by getting whooped by my great aunt. Yes, aunt Nancy worked at the same school I went to, and therefore I wasn't just the joker; I was the batman as well. I had to be sneaky in my class clown behaviors.

I vividly remember once getting bold because my aunt wasn't at the school that day. Chewing gum and mouthing off the substitute teacher, I was making everyone laugh. "Bubble gum, you're hilarious," said a friend. Giggles kept rolling as I kept giving the poor substitute teacher a tough time, and then suddenly, everyone stopped.

All I heard was a low whisper, "oh no, bubblegum..." And I looked at the doorway, and right there stood aunt Nancy. She gave me a good whooping right there in front of everyone. And when I returned home, I had my mouth washed with soap so I would remember not to mouth off. And that's when I learned my lesson: if you're going to be a clown, you better not get caught.

A Tale of Two AccidentS

Chapter Four

If there's one thing worth remembering, it is that no matter what your life's condition is, you must always be ready to open the doors ahead of you. Unfortunately, there are doors behind you that you must close first. That's a general philosophy of life, but I got to see its literal impact first hand. When my brother forgot to close the door, I fell out of the car we were riding in.

I woke up a survivor. I did not understand that a car had run over me, and I had dodged certain death. I was only aware of the concerned and loving company around me. When you go through such an experience as a child, it transforms you. You develop a different appreciation for life and heightened caution regarding chaos.

Kids grow up not knowing the uncertainty that adults feel regarding finances, food on the table, and their relationships. But I grew up too quickly when I went through not one but two physical accidents. Once I was en route to our church. And from my perspective, I blacked out and heard the preacher telling my aunt that I would need elaborate stitches. It turned out that it was the surgeon, and I had been in the hospital for a while.

These two accidents, albeit six years apart, brought me to the same place: a place where I examined life from a sublime distance. I got to see the fragility of our species by examining myself as the specimen. I could hear the cries of my mother and the concern of my aunt.

The lady who would shut the door if you didn't come home in time was not too sure of her rules and view of the world. Everyone had the ground taken from underneath their feet. Such moments bring us to sober moments of reflection. If we are lucky, they leave us with a realization or a lesson that can help us in the future.

I had already dodged getting teased as "shorty" by being the funny guy my peers wanted to laugh with. Was I going to be able to walk again, or would I become different in yet another way? As a child, these questions are quite important. They are important even as a teenager or as an adult.

You would think the physical pain would consume my mind so totally that I would not have any room to ponder the future and how my life would be affected. For some reason, there was a numbness that took over. Most of the pain at this point was psychological.

Resentment and anger bubbled in me because I had given up my freedom in order to be protected. That was the unspoken deal: I'll live in your bubble, and you'll keep me from getting hurt.

But the chaos of life had found its way to me despite my aunt coddling me and treating me like fragile porcelain. 'ENOUGH,' I thought. At that moment, that was the only word consuming my mind. 'ENOUGH.' I have had enough of this monitoring and bubble wrapping. There, I decided that I'll do my best to venture out of the protective bubble every chance I got.

Recipe for Joy

Chapter Five

You have previously read about my attempts to try and fit in. For me, life was so much about running away from getting teased or hurt that I had never stopped and thought about happiness. To some extent, I had no idea I could be happy. And that's where my internal transformation played the biggest role. My life after that "enough is enough" moment changed.

I became a rebel of sorts and derived pleasure from getting away with things I knew aunt Nancy didn't approve of. Among those was smoking grass. You would think that a kid who was around a mother with drug issues would know a thing or two about drugs. No sir! The first time I smoked grass, I actually rolled up real grass and tried to smoke it. I can't even write about that without cracking up. We eventually got to the other grass, my friends and I, but I discovered something deeply profound in the process.

Joy comes not from obeying or breaking the rules; it comes from the life you build with your friends. Too many people are focused on one of three goals. They want to make a lot of money or be really famous. And if it's neither of those, then they most likely want to be with a specific guy or girl. But most of your joy will never come from any of these goals.

True happiness comes from having friends you enjoy the company of. And that's what I found transitioning junior high. From kindergarten to second-grade was brutal. And from second to sith, there was a transition from a segregated black-only group to a mixed classroom. That was different and took some getting used to. But by the time I was in junior high, I had people I was already familiar with studying in the same class.

School life was no longer about running away from teasing. It wasn't about breaking into a new social group. The pupils in junior high who knew each other from previous classes all found familiarity and comfort in each other.

Once I was no longer focusing on the fact that I was "different," I could begin to have fun. And I discovered that I was great at having fun. I had previously adopted others' view of me. They looked at me as if I could not be as happy as other kids. And for some reason, I never disagreed. But finding myself in the company of friends who didn't treat me like fragile decor helped me see past the assumed fragility of my condition.

This is what I consider my "coming out of my shell" stage. I started enjoying life more, and once I had more to live for, I had more to fight for. So many people are chained to their cubicles, working jobs they hate. Of course, they don't want to fight for their company or fulfill its mission: they don't enjoy what they do. I took this lesson seriously: you have to find enjoyment in what you do or stop doing it because life is too short to live any other way!

Spirituality and Slipping

Chapter Six

People don't understand that being spiritual and being a great student doesn't go hand in hand. Since spiritual people are often called "good," and bad students are called "bad," the general notion is that if you took a priest, a hermit, and a monk and put them in a classroom, they would all be perfect students. In reality, they would probably chill in the backbenches while discussing God and scripture. I was a good student. Initially, I would get good grades, but by the time I was in 9th, I was a straight-up honors student.

Many would assume that being a good student would have a generally "good" impact on one's life. Unfortunately, that's not true. I tied being a good student to being a good person because that's how Aunt Nancy seemed to see things. Consequently, when my grades would slip, I would also build up guilt around the school.

I was church-going. I was religious, yet my "devilishness" in school (which peaked around 10th grade) would keep me from being content with my spiritual path. Nancy had baptized me at five, and while I was into it, it was her decision and was more about the general traditions of my great aunt's household. But in high school, I developed a crush on a girl and started visiting her church.

At the same time, I was maintaining attendance at my church. You often hear about people working two jobs; I was doing two church shifts. And though the beginning of this interest was more to do with the company I kept, I developed a deeper connection with the lord through this. I see this as the beginning of my Pentecostal life if we're talking figuratively.

But while this was happening on the spiritual level, I was also keeping up my antics at school. I wasn't at the school my aunt worked at during the time, but the security guard knew my aunt and her relatives. The guard seemed to know aunties I didn't even know I had. But I never thought my aunt would find out. Yes, the school system encourages snitching but come on, who would go out of their way to get in touch with my busy aunt Nancy and let her know I was skipping classes to sit in sessions with substitute teachers. Who would tell her I was going to my lunch and my friends' lunch while bailing on classes? Apparently, someone did.

Because I remember getting my name called over the PA system, I was instructed to visit the principal's office. And I walk in to find a very angry Aunt Nancy sitting there. I got scolded to kingdom come, and that was the end of school for me. I did not finish high school.

But going full circle, we return to the idea of spirituality and slipping. I slipped in school but had retained my spiritual self. That helped me to a degree. But there was some serious guilt associated with not finishing school. Had I not seen myself as a bad person, I might have skipped emotional torture. But perhaps the torture was what made me take the next steps.

Getting the High out of High School

Chapter Seven

I have had a share of experiences with drugs. I've been around them, and in some parts of my life, I've actually abused them. It started with seeing my mom get hooked. Then I had friends who weren't priest material, though, towards the beginning of my double-church phase, I weaned them off. IF anything, that's what kept me from throwing my life to drugs and crime when I dropped out of high school. It was a low point, at least from the perspective of someone who went from being an honors student to being a high school dropout.

I had a lot to be angry about, starting with the insecurities discussed in chapter one. Remember, I wasn't feeling like the king of the hill when my younger brother was allowed to ride bikes and sent to an expensive school while I only sat in the wagon and got to go to a significantly lower-tier school from a syllabus and budget perspective.

Even so, I managed to get great grades, only to be stopped by my personality not matching what the school system wanted. So what if I wanted to have fun? Was it so big a crime that I should be plagued by the consequences of not even graduating high school? At this point in my life, I couldn't even get a job at McDonald's, and my aunt Nancy wasn't about to re-visit her view of the world to accommodate my point of view.

From her perspective, I messed up by not being the robot who sits through all the classes seeking nothing but knowledge. And now I had to pitch in with the bills. Fortunately, that's where I found out about the Job Corps, pretty much the only opportunity open for me. I discuss this later at length in the chapter that follows.

I want to use the rest of this chapter to emphasize my point regarding what motivates drug use. In my life, drugs became a way to hide from the pain. And most of this pain was completely avoidable had the grown-ups made an effort to see things from my perspective. They didn't need to agree. All I desired was to be understood. If you're reading this book and you're a youngster, please remember that you have positives alongside your negatives. Even if the elders keep bringing up these negatives, please don't let that build this negative image that you end up actualizing.

Take a moment and re-calibrate. Make a list of your positives and read it over and over. If you see yourself as a bad person, you'll allow yourself to become a bad person.

And if you're an adult reading this, please remember to keep perspective regarding the youngsters' positives. Let them know when they do things right, not just when they mess up. And try to understand them because drugs, violence, and crimes are just a manifestation of teenagers accepting that they are bad people. And no one can convince them they are bad except the adults whose approval they seek.

Second Chance

Chapter Eight

There's a sobering thought in our scripture that many of us fail to reflect on. The resurrection of our lord and savior, Jesus Christ. This motif, alongside the second coming, represent something we must examine in our own lives: second chances. From Noah's arc to Jesus rising up after his crucifixion, there's a consistent thread of God giving a second chance to his chosen ones. Even returning to the old testament, we have the story of God giving a second chance to the people that Moses led out of Egypt.

This means that anytime you feel like you get a second chance at life, you must see it as God's work and ponder the purpose of said chance. There are two types of second chances. One is where you have a close brush with death but manage to come out alive. This has nothing to do with your role in the process. You might have been nearly hit by a car or mugged at gunpoint but managed to live. This is similar to the second life granted to Jesus. He wasn't at fault for his death. But there's also another kind of second chance: the one where you get to recover after messing up.

That's shown in God forgiving Moses' people after they worshiped a false god. In your life, this could be something like messing with drugs but managing to come out of the experience without losing everything.

I had both kinds of second chances. I got run over by a car and once fell and hit my head on the rocks by the side of the road. I got a second chance at life two times between those two accidents (discussed earlier in this book).

But I also got a second chance when I discovered the Job Corps. I had dropped out of high school and was on the road to failing at life. Even minimum wage jobs required a high school graduate-level education. But once I got my chance with the Job Corps, I had a sense that this was the lord's work and that I had to try my best to make something of myself. I picked business administration. I had always wanted to get a business education and a computer-related degree. Now I had my chance to learn in an active manner that complimented my personality.

Half a year in, I got into a fight with a guy about a girl. Needless to say, I got suspended. Before I could step back and see what happened, the negative monologue was already revving up. "Oh, Jerry, you're the black sheep of your family. They were right not to get you into a good school in the first place."

I was so demoralized that I didn't even go to the disciplinary committee's hearing. That led to what would become a permanent suspension of sorts. I messed with drugs, and shortly after, got suicidal. One day I remember sitting and contemplating suicide when I heard a voice. "I need you to do great work. I have great things planned for you," it said. I looked around. There were only dogs in that area, and that voice for sure wasn't that of a dog. I didn't hear it with my ears. I heard it with my whole being. I was saved by the voice of God.

A Second Life

Chapter Nine

From my perspective, the moment God took the idea of suicide out of my heart, he granted me a second life. This was more than a second chance. Had I gone ahead, this chapter wouldn't be written. The book would end with the last one, and I'm glad it didn't. I poured my entire self-discipline, willpower, and potential towards a single goal: do something worthy of a second chance at life. There are trillions to one odds of each one of us being born. And to be born again the way I did requires significant luck.

I returned to the Job Corps, and they took me back. They could see it in my eyes: I was a changed man. They put me on academic probation, which is fair enough for someone who had gotten into a fight and skipped the hearing committee's hearing. I kept my focus on my studies and personal development. Soon, I was in a supervisory role where I could even take students to church with me. In that capacity, I learned that true leadership is never about what you can do. It is about what you should do.

Those who know me understand that I have always been an empath, and my people-pleasing tendencies shifted with my new responsibilities. I wasn't trying to make people laugh. I was trying to help them get a better connection with God. Most people do not realize how much those closer to crime and sin need God. Priests and pastors alike are a little guilty of preaching to the choir. Those closest to drugs and street violence rarely get the kind of attention they need from a man of God.

I genuinely believe churches must actively work to bring drug users and jobless people into their fold. Anyone who is significantly vulnerable needs the community and spiritual connection provided by a church. With the job corps, I brought people who needed financial and career security closer to God. There is nothing more significant than spiritual security.

If you're expecting this story to continue going the path of me being a great student and acing the game of life, you've not been paying attention. Of course, my strictly academic phase fell off as I started slipping again. But this time, there was one factor distinctly different from the other times: I didn't see myself as a bad person.

I had the opportunity to do so much good in my time at the Job Corps that I understood that slacking on studies didn't make me a bad guy. I didn't get my GED, but I graduated with my business administration degree. I remember my aunt at the graduation. She asked me if I was going to return home. Of course, I wasn't. I had to try my hand at life and get a job to pay my bills. I lived in multiple shared settings during this phase of my life. But ultimately, I'm content that I did not waste my second life.

Shifting Environment

Chapter Ten

You may remember that I opened this book with thoughts on the impact of one's environment on their character. Well, I certainly experienced a shift when I lived with different housemates at different times in my life. I would consider my brother as my first housemate as we grew up in our great aunt's house.

This is akin to living with someone who is treated better than you. This can stoke the fires of resentment and make you extremely insecure. At another time, I lived with my cousin. And when you live with someone who needs help, you can build self-confidence if you're the type of person who helps. But you must be careful not to try to save people who don't want to save themselves. That will only cause resentment and frustration.

I didn't know if someone was going to rob her or if she was going to rob somebody. She was hooked on heroin, and you can imagine that life was pretty chaotic around her. I spent days between states of protective worry and initiative. Alongside my job corps responsibilities, I helped her rear her child despite her heroin addiction. This was nowhere near the picture of "normal" many people have in their minds. I'm glad I was there because I was trained not to put "normalcy" on a pedestal.

Nobody treated me as normal growing up, and it helped me be comfortable in this novel environment of helping people addicted to drugs get clean. I was also aware of the impact of judgment on one's psyche and self-image. That's why I let go of my judgmental instincts during this period.

I helped her and some others with an open heart and an open mind and saw how fundamental their transformation was. It was the first time I was seeing someone's life get better in front of my eyes because of the effort I was putting in.

This was different from the times I had made people laugh and seen them be happy for a moment. This was equivalent to helping them once and seeing them be better off forever.

Of course, I'm not implying that my cousin's life became perfect after that. My point is that the way I made a difference ended up counting in the long run. And here I found what I wanted to do with my life: make a lasting impact on others.

The Darker Side of ReSponSibility

Chapter Eleven

In the previous chapter, I showed the positive side of my time taking care of someone addicted to drugs. I did so because it is my firm belief that we must always count the positive with the negative. My earlier insecurities emerged from grownups making me feel bad for my behavior at school without putting enough emphasis on my good grades.

I wasn't going to do that with myself as an adult. Sure, I was a young adult and was getting involved with drugs, but I was helping people and doing my best. But counting positives doesn't mean airbrushing the negatives.

And what started as the responsible thing to do quickly morphed into a nightmare. It was a classic case of becoming the thing you set out to destroy. To put things in context, I did not want to go to North Carolina. I didn't want to be in the protective and stern shadow of aunt Nancy, but Nancy did not prepare me to be independent.

Add to that the burden of having no job and living with a cousin hooked on drugs; I was tempted to get involved with drugs myself. One day, I had such a bad fall because of loose infrastructure in the place where I lived that I broke my arm. From elbow onward, it was quite a horrific sight.

I remember waking up in the hospital to see my great aunt by the bedside. She was on her way for a different drop-off. It seemed like God was not only watching over me but was making a point of keeping Nancy close. She stuck around for a few days, but I, too, stuck to my guns.

I was going to build a life in North Carolina, and I was going to do it by myself. I bit off more than I could chew. When I got out of the hospital, I still had a broken arm, albeit it was in a better position and en route to recovery. Aside from having a broken arm, I did not have a place to live.

The place where I had my accident, I had to move out of. That's because I was suing them, and aunt Nancy helped with hiring a lawyer. Away from that place, I didn't even have a job to put a different roof over my head. So I lived with my two sisters. Both of their houses were in the projects and meant only for them. So I had to sneak in and keep a low profile as I lived there.

During this time, I began doing drugs. Soon that turned to drug dealing. I needed God again, and had I slipped on my promises to my fellow man as much as I did with God, I would have no company. But I am quite glad God pulled me out of that dark place. That said, it wasn't exactly the smoothest way to pull someone out of that life. It was a close call, and you'll see how in the next chapter.

A Tale of Two Police EncounterS

Chapter Twelve

I have no criminal record, and if I had one, I would not have become a deacon. And while many of us take for granted our lack of criminal record, it isn't obvious why we shouldn't be thankful for avoiding trouble. If you've broken the law but managed not to get caught, you should be thankful and see it as a second chance. And if you've not broken laws, then you should be glad circumstances have kept you from that life altogether.

I remember once having an argument with my aunt because I wanted to go hang out at my friend's place. She didn't allow it, and I was so angry. "How can you decide such things for me?" I said as I walked to my room. I had a tight frown on my face, the kind that would give you early wrinkles. I was so full of rebellious rage that I kept tossing and turning in the bed and couldn't even sleep.

But soon, I woke up to an eye-opener: the place I wanted to go to got raided by the police. Had I been there, I would have had a criminal record. And at that time, my rebellious rage was calmed, and I developed temporary respect for my aunt's authority and wisdom despite being pretty much a grownup in my own eyes. Only now can I see the true value of not having a police record.

The second close call was much closer and of higher consequences. Remember how I chronologically narrated my life to the point of living with two different sisters? Well, around this time, I was living in the house with my mom's sister. My friend, the one I sold drugs with, was with me when there was a loud knock on the door.

It would be unfair to call it a knock. It was more like someone practicing his boxing chops on the door. Upon opening, we found out it was the police. Five officers at least entered to look for the dealer's brother.

They were looking for a gun, and that means turning everything around. And I had two bags of powder in my pockets. I went towards the bathroom to flush the drugs, but there already was a policeman there. There were policemen at every door. But because they were focused on finding this guy or a gun, they tunnel-visioned on their mission and missed out on a drug bust. And boy, am I glad they did. Right after they left, I said, 'this is it.' I dropped the begs and decided never to touch or push drugs again. And that's where I turned my life around.

FaSt Food and Chicken WingS

Chapter Thirteen

By now, you know my journey up to the point of taking a minimum-wage job at Hardee's. It is a story worth telling because the next time you see someone working as a barista or another service job, and they're in their young adult years, don't see them as upstarts. They've lived a life that has brought them there, and they have a path ahead of them that you cannot predict or judge.

I took up a job at Hardee's and started earning some money. I was simultaneously saving up to get my own place, even if on rent and not as a mortgage. I wanted to be away from rugs and other negative influences. You can almost see the improvement in humility. At one point, I thought I was going to be the person saving others from drug use. Now I knew better.

I had to be away from that environment to do anything about the drug problem in my community. During this time, my Aunt

Nancy's neighbor introduced me to Pastor Gillis. Pastor Gillis' church was much more interesting then Aunt Nancy's. I guess it had to do with the age group. Too many old people hung out at Aunt Nancy's church, and as a result, it was pretty dry.

At my new church, I could see the vigor and, more importantly, something that would sufficiently engage me to keep me away from drugs and other problematic behavior. At one point, Pastor Gillis asked me to step up with my responsibilities at the church.

"How do you expect me to do that? I ain't a preacher," I protested.

"I'll take you under my wing," she assured me.

I had no idea what that even meant. I was just thinking, 'You aren't a chicken." She did take me under her wing and helped me get more active in my Christian work. I got my next baptism around then. It was the mama chicken's idea as she made a valid point: my baptism at five wasn't of my own choosing. This was a very rigorous period that tested the limits of what I could do. I remember working at Hardee's being there before 10:45 to prepare for the 11 O clock shift. And soon after getting my shut-eye and being at the church in my work clothes.

There were some serious "shut and pray" sessions where you were on your knees or had your face to the floor throughout the night. Yet, I breezed through all of it with ease: this was the first indicator that I had found my calling. Unlike school or Job Corps, I wasn't disengaged or needed to exert my energy elsewhere. I was content and even had some upward mobility as I got to extend my leadership beyond the levels I had practiced at Job Corps.

Furthermore, I got to do more and be more. I had my own place, and I was en route to my deaconship. And till then, working a fast-food job, being under the right-wing, and overseeing drums and keyboards in my Hardee's uniform seemed like the perfect routine.

Deacon Jerry

Chapter Fourteen

In the year 94, I became a Deacon. I had to appear in front of a board, and there was a formal process. They don't just let anyone become a deacon. One of the requirements is that the individual doesn't have a criminal record. Well, I did have a history of questionable behavior, but none of it was on the record. So fortunately for me, I met their standards and was made a Deacon.

This is significant because, to me, it signaled elevation in my climb towards doing more of God's work. My aunt's church was an eccentric one, to say the least. It was a small ministry. My aunt was a pastor, and her mother was a pastor too. Another member of the family was involved, too, but she wanted to just run things and had little interest in the spiritual side of it. And for the sake of her privacy, I would rather not specify her t this stage.

From being the black sheep of the family to being entrusted with this role, I had come a long way, and I was proud of it. I was even doing some accounting duties for my aunt. Remember, I had business administration education, and that came in handy when I chased her up with a few hundred dollars that were missing here and there. I must say I was much more persistent than my aunt in this regard. It only fits then that she took it in a stride while I was the one given the charge to keep track of this.

I remember one day just sitting in my apartment and thinking about my past, and suddenly tears began streaming down my face. I had remembered one of the lowest points of my life and how God had come through for me even then.

If you remember the chapter where I discuss having no roof over my head and a broken arm with no job, you will know at which phase in my life this happened. I was at the lowest rungs of poverty then and was searching through trash to find something I could eat.

I prayed to God for a hot meal. And walking back, I noticed church's chicken. It was in a mall, and I walked into the mall as if being guided there. I knew I didn't have money for the meal. Suddenly there was a knock on the window. I turned around, and it was a member of the church.

They asked me how I was, and I was already semi-high. Remember, at this stage of my life, I was into drugs. They told me I should get my act together. And I listened and nodded. They asked me if I wanted to eat. And it smelt good, but I had to say no for appearance's sake. Thank God they offered me money to buy some food elsewhere. And that night, I slept with a hot meal in my belly.

Now I was thinking back to that day. God hadn't abandoned me there. I had just stopped believing in myself, from there to being a deacon with my own place and income. I had come a long way.

HintS of a Gift

Chapter Fifteen

One would think that my life's standards would rise after becoming a deacon. If my life were that simple, it would be too boring for a book. Slightly prior to my deaconship, I got the hints of a gift. I started speaking in tongues on occasion. I still remember vividly how bizarre the experience was: I was saying things that made perfect sense to me yet sounded like they were in a completely foreign language. I would have thought I was crazy ha I not connected the dots.

I was beginning to see a direct connection with the Lord. from communicating with the apostles to hearing God speak; I had been exposed to flashes of divine rapport, yet I did not have around me one person I could share this with.

While my Pastor was quite a fun pastor in her own right, her ministry wasn't the kind that would accommodate such experiences. She, too, wouldn't understand. And that's why I kept it all to myself. In hindsight, that was the single biggest mistake of my life. It is selfish to hold back the word of God because you're afraid people will think you're crazy. And bottling up this "gift" drove me to yet another slump. And it manifested with my return to Connecticut.

Across the next few chapters, you'll notice a roller-coaster of random events rich with tragedy and surprises. They will all seem random till you notice that God was pushing me through all facets of life till I could come back and face my gift. I firmly believe that had I been open about my gift right away, I would have suffered significant pain, but it would have faded away. Instead, I kept running from the gift and accumulated enough pain till I couldn't take it anymore.

It first started with a harmless visit to Connecticut. It was genuinely supposed to be a visit, and had I kept my humility and believed that going back to that environment will hurt me; I wouldn't have even stepped in that direction.

However, I was in Connecticut and ended up staying with my cousin. Previously I had a fall there, and now I was staying with her, and she had more kids than before. I was "welcome" but with double-quotes.

I could hear them be concerned about the food I was eating. I did not have a job because when you move states, Hardee's doesn't keep your spot open for you to return months later. More importantly, it isn't a paid vacation.

Because of my hand, it was tougher for me to get a job. I moved out of my cousin's place and lived with an older sister. She, too, couldn't host me for long because of the projects' lease restrictions. For a while, I stayed with my middle sister only to have to move out because of how painful it was to watch her boyfriend mistreat her. Of course, I was going to intervene upon seeing him take drugs in front of the kids. But as a guest, how long would I be welcome if I did this? Exactly. I ended up staying with my grandmother eventually, but in the meantime, I had slipped and started visiting strip clubs.

Deacon Jerry, Part 2

Chapter Sixteen

I had never stayed with my grandmother before, and she had some serious old people rules. You would have to be home by seven and sleep because she would be asleep by seven. The entire paradigm of my life took a significant shift. But before living with my grandmother, I had gotten back en route to deaconship. By now, you can notice that despite executing self-sabotaging measures, I ended up returning to the origins where my gift awaited.

There was a church next door to my sister's, and I started visiting. The deacon there took me under his wings and prepared me for deaconship. You may be thinking, 'Wait a minute, Jerry, weren't you already a deacon?' I was but not here. I got ordained by a different church and was in a different state. So I studied with this deacon and stayed with him in the summer of 1995.

Flash forward to living with my grandma and her strict rules; I couldn't handle that as an adult in my early twenties. Fortunately, I had gotten closer to God and once found myself shut in and praying. God, I know this isn't the life you have planned for me.

Everything seemed so scattered and disorganized. Church work, borderline homelessness, close calls with drugs, and seeing domestic abuse upfront were all things that didn't make sense together. So I knew there was something wrong that I wanted to make right.

And that's when I heard the voice tell me I have to return to North Carolina. What do I have to do now? Yes, I had to return to North Carolina, but I didn't have any money. Asking grandma for money with the promise and intentions of returning it, I explained that I was supposed to return to North Carolina.

She agreed. As a wiser person, she knew the effects of the environment and wanted me to move away from who I was in earlier stages of my life. And the best way to do that was to remove me from an environment that had such a strong negative influence. So I returned to North Carolina only to find out that my previous pastor was dealing with so much in her life that she didn't have time to take on projects with me. However, the lady was kind enough to hand me off to her cousin (also a pastor), so we could continue the Lord's work.

By now, you can see that I was definitely closer to acknowledging the gift and using it, but I still wasn't quite there.

There was substantial pain I had to go through to realize what should be singularly focused on. The next few chapters outline the journey to that realization.

Girl ProblemS

Chapter Seventeen

They say no man's story is complete without girl troubles. If that is true, a certain part of me wishes my story had remained incomplete. One of the most painful periods of life started off quite smoothly. I met a girl and ended up staying with her godmother. It's worth noting that though I had visited strip clubs before, it was more of an exercise in rebellion and boundaries than a sexual thing. I had touched most vices with curiosity more than intention. So at 27, I was still a virgin. And most of you would know that in such a position, your human side is vulnerable to emotional entrapment even though your spiritual side may be elevated.

That's why for those saving themselves, it is often recommended to avoid getting trapped in relationships outside marriage. If you get sexual before marriage at a late enough age, you can easily get manipulated. And therefore, if you're saving yourself, you should truly go the length and get intimate only after marriage.

I couldn't do that, and we ended up together. Though we did eventually marry, it seemed like we were only amplifying the wrong. Her family did not like me and weren't supportive of this marriage. Her pastor wasn't okay with it, nor was mine. My aunt said she wouldn't even visit or send a kind word because she didn't approve of the girl.

But being young, we did what we thought was best and ended up getting married. Neither side would host us as a couple because my family didn't like her, and her family wasn't cheering for me, so we ended up living separately, her with mother and me with my aunt. We would get together like teenagers. And honestly, that was probably the first sign that what we were doing was wrong.

At this point, life got so chaotic that I kept thinking, what was there worth living for? And in hindsight, I believe it was God making me see that nothing else except my mission was worth living for; that I had to dedicate my life to that one thing. But while I was there at that moment, I could not see it.

Still, 96 wasn't all bad: I got ordained as a prophet. Interestingly, you'll notice that whenever I took a step in the right direction, life would get more organized. The year following that, I got my first trailer. I had never imagined myself as a trailer park resident, but there I was. And honestly, it was better than living under someone else's roof. At least now I was the man of the house.

But I still couldn't get a job. I worked small jobs, but nothing sustainable would come my way because of my hand. You can't do a lot with one hand pretty much broken. So I ended up getting on disability in the year 98. and that's when things again started to take the wrong turn.

Freeing LimitationS

Chapter Eighteen

There was a lot of drama in the year 98. It started with arguments and escalated to me getting hit. I tried my best to defend myself, but there's only so much you can do to protect yourself without physically restraining or pushing the other person. I firmly believe that once that physical fighting boundary is crossed, a relationship is going to get worse. But I didn't know it at the time. There were periods of extreme warmth and coldness.

I knew I was being cheated on but didn't want to face it. And while I suppressed my disapproval, it built up resentment in me. This resentment would come out through passive-aggressiveness. The year went by, and I did not file for a divorce. However, I started distancing myself from my wife. And, of course, with every step in the right direction, my life improved. So guess what happened when I stepped away from my abusive and cheating partner? I got blessed with a car.

This was the year 2000, and I had gotten an apartment in 99. So things were looking up till I got my spinal stenosis diagnosis. Doctors told me my back was curving in a way that was compressing my spine. I had to get back surgery. In the meantime, marital life wasn't going anywhere either. I remember getting together with my wife only for her to confess she cheated after we got intimate.

I already knew this on some level, so I wasn't shocked, but this led the relationship to open up slightly. Now I was presented with the option to have threesomes. I thought it would be a harmless, fun one-time thing, but it somehow became a triangular relationship on its own. Getting in bed with two women became the norm for a significant period since.

In 2001, I was driving back late with my gospel music on and was so exhausted that I pretty much dozed off. In other words, I was sleeping. Consequently, my car ended up on the other side of the road. I'm glad there was no traffic, or I would have been in a terrible accident. Instead, I was in a slightly less terrible accident as the car ended up in a ditch.

I was naive enough to crank my engine, and only God protected me from the potential blast that could have happened. You should never rev the engine if your car has crashed. I got out and threw dirt around, trying to stop a car to help me. No one stopped. I looked back at my totaled car and felt bad: it was given to me by the pastor and was a sweet ride. Fortunately, someone eventually stopped. It was a policewoman! "Sir, are you drunk?" she asked with concern in her voice. "No, ma'am, I was just getting off work late," I explained. I returned home safely, and all of this was starting to take a toll on my body. Little did I know that things were about to get really interesting.

Limiting FreedomS

Chapter Nineteen

I found myself back in Connecticut for a visit. This was the year 2002 following the accident where I had totaled my first car. It was also when an apartment upstairs caught fire, and the sprinklers destroyed our place. Knowing this, you can see the rest of the events that unfolded in Connecticut as logical chaos. For a brief period, we lived in shelters, and I did eventually move to a second trailer. My arguments with my wife had also reached a boiling point, and finding not even a moment of peace; I took pills.

When I did this, it was with every intention of killing myself, but I hadn't taken nearly enough. When they got me to the hospital, they didn't even need to pump my stomach; I hadn't taken enough pills to cause serious harm; I had only taken enough to expose myself as a danger to myself.

They told me they would need to commit me to a psych ward. "I will never go to a psych ward," I protested. To this, they responded with the other option: going to jail. If I didn't agree to check in at a psych ward, I would end up in jail. Upon hearing this, I said, "well, to the psych ward I go."

It was a different environment, to say the least. You couldn't be near a blade and hence couldn't shave. No one had belts for obvious reasons. During the brief periods of contact with the outside world, I found out over the telephone that the things I was trying to escape from were persisting in the world. My partner didn't show concern over what I had done and kept up what had initially brought me to the point of no return.

This gave me the opportunity to display sobriety and self-control. Consequently, I was out of the psych ward and back to normal life, whatever normal meant for me. During this period, I had a job and, in fact, was the only one working. I stayed with my sister, and she had kids, lots of them.

Then my partner had kids as well. There were plenty of mouths to feed, and I was the only one working. Perhaps this is what initially triggered the carelessness that led to yet another accident. In the year 2005, I was en route to pick up my lover's kids when I got into an accident. We soon got cleared out of the hospital, but I could notice some serious issues that I was confident would persist.

SeriouS ConSequenceS

Chapter Twenty

Perhaps hospitals clear you because they want vacant beds, or perhaps I genuinely was fine for a while. All I know is that the days following the accident, I could see some serious issues. The chief among these was the washroom issue. Not only did it hurt when I went to the washroom but my voluntary control over those bodily functions wavered. Many people take for granted their control over their own bowel movements and urination.

At that moment, I learned that this was nothing to take for granted. I remember my legs giving way just walking down the stairs. When I knew something was seriously wrong, I returned to the hospital. It took two visits for them to finally acknowledge that I have a problem. And when they realized there was an issue, they also understood how serious of an issue this was.

Soon, I had an IV stuck in my neck as doctors pondered how to best deal with my case. Eventually, they came to a consensus and sent me off to Chapel Hill, North Carolina. I was told that my spine was getting worse that I would need yet another surgery.

I was paralyzed from the waist down and couldn't see my son even though he wanted to see me. His mother kept him from visiting. My aunt couldn't keep me company through this ordeal. I was fighting this alone till I realized I didn't have to.

I returned to God and repented. I repented because I didn't know what else I could do. He had given me so many chances, and I had kept slipping. More than my legs back, I prayed to have a sense of purpose and clarity of thought. I prayed for the pain to stop affecting me on a psychological level.

One day the doctor walked up to me and said, "I regret to inform you, sir, that we don't know what to do." then he paused. A million thoughts raced through my head. What does one do when those who are best equipped to solve a problem say they don't know what to do? What was to become of me? Getting a job was hard with my arm condition alone; now, the current situation would complicate things further.

My thoughts were interrupted as the doctor continued, "...but I know you are a man of faith." And that returned me to a place of calm. I wasn't going to make it all come together; it was God who was going to do it. All I had to do was have faith. And strangely enough, this is the period where I developed the rock-solid belief that no matter what happens in life, I will be fine.

Zero Comfort

Chapter Twenty-One

Time is indiscriminate; it doesn't pause when you get hurt. The world keeps revolving because it never revolved around you, to begin with. But what if the world is something you pick up on your shoulders?

I had serious responsibilities at this stage of my life and yet was in such a bad condition that I couldn't trust myself to return to consciousness if I slept. I remember sleeping once only to come to life seconds before the emergency room technicians were about to hit me with some electricity to restart my heart.

But as I said, the world doesn't stop revolving. My sister lost her baby during this time. And soon after, she lost her life. My mother, who was still on drugs, found out about this and got clean enough to make sense of things. Soon, she reached out to me, and as I picked up the phone, I had a million thoughts in my head. There was a lot I wanted to say, but before I could say anything, she unloaded her guilt.

"Both my oldest babies are going through it," she said, "and I wasn't there for her and can't be there for you. I wasn't there for you when you were young," she sobbed. Instead of getting comfort, I ended up being the one comforting her. In my head, I was reviewing the film of my life, the accidents, the insecurities, feeling neglected, trying to prove that I was worthy, and constantly competing with my brother. All of that came to mind hearing my mom speak. I wanted to tell her that I wished things had been different. But telling her wouldn't have made things different. We were where we were. And there was not much I could do about that now, could I?

I told her it was alright and that she did the best she could for us. And that her being around in her condition would have hurt us. None of this lent me any comfort. As far as I was concerned, I was still alone. And only my faith in God was keeping me up.

They couldn't keep me at the hospital for long. The paycheck has to return home. And when I was back at the house, one would think I would have some support and understanding. Wrong. It was everything as it was, except my health was in a bad position.

Zero Support

Chapter Twenty-Two

I am going to say it: I deserved better. It took me a long time to realize that I deserved to be treated better than I was. As a people pleaser, I had looked at things from others' perspective too much and, in the process, forgotten to think about myself.

I deserved better than to be abandoned. I deserved better than to be cheated on. I deserved better than to be neglected despite being the sole breadwinner. But I am glad I never hung my hat on life's unfairness. Life is unfair, but so what? This is the only shot you have of making an impact. And ironically, it took multiple broken bones for me to realize the importance of the soul. My fifth accident and how I was treated afterward opened my eyes to my own interests.

I cooked, cleaned, and paid the bills. What was everyone else doing? I deserved better but just saying that wouldn't change anything. Now more than ever, I realized the need for action. So much of my misery was coming from being okay with being miserable.

We were taught to take our problems to the lord and just pray. And for a while, that's what I did. I was buying a house for my family, but there were too many people living there. I was unable to do anything after the accident and what I did a lot of was crying.

I had to sob at night as I had to put a happy face for the world during the day. The worst part about all this was the loneliness. I advise people reading this book to reach out to people they know are going through it.

Make sure your friends know they can talk to you. Sharing the problem eases half the burden. So please do not let self-absorption and immediate issues get in the way of connection. Most of the emotional burden of my sister's passing could have been relieved had I someone to grieve with. But I couldn't go due to my condition and was instead left with a thankless household.

I was alone thinking about the times where we connected. I helped her with her first child, as you may recall from earlier chapters; I walked her down the aisle. This period is what I call my painful July. Towards the end, another bizarre thing happened.

The ex-wife was cleaning the bedroom one night. And since I slept mighty late that evening, I was awake enough to get curious. She was taking everything from the bedroom and putting it in the empty bedroom. What's going on? I wake up in the middle of the night, and there's music turned up, and she's in the bedroom. We still lived together back then. My son walks with me, but because I was outside and not with his mom, he didn't knock. Instead of knocking on the door, he walks into the bedroom and then walks out immediately. There was someone else in there with her.

Welcome to My Love Life

Chapter Twenty-Three

I had been cheated on before in my life but learning that I was being disrespected and disregarded when I was paralyzed caused a visceral wound in me. After that, I was emotionally turned off and away from relationships and love. Some part of me was open to the idea of love, but I did not meet any women with that in my heart.

After this, it was more about benefits and sex. And while many may judge me for it, I am not telling my story to get a pass from anyone. The entire point of telling my story is that I am human and have survived a lot. That incident caused more damage than most of my physical accidents because physical accidents are restrained: they're within the bounds of one's own body. When I was paralyzed, for instance, it didn't even inconvenience many people as no one had to sit by my bedside. On the other hand, when I received this emotional wound, I turned to playboy antics, and I'm sure a lot of women were emotionally hurt by that.

The only break I remember from such life was when I moved to a nursing home because of my condition. I wasn't crazy, yet I had been in a psych ward. And now I wasn't old but was in a nursing home. It seems like God was putting me in such drastically different positions in life so I could learn and cultivate the ability to connect with anyone.

I wasn't at my best relationship with God, I must admit, yet I had many blessings. I could hold a one-hour conversation with a pastor, connect on a deeply sexual level with a girl who couldn't spell Jesus, talk to people twice my age, and play with those quarter my age. At the nursing home, I also met Steve, who went on to play a bigger role in my social life.

While I could connect on an emotional level with people of all ages, I didn't have much of a sexual appetite for any residents of the nursing home. That was a nice break from the kind of rampage I would have gone on otherwise. But jokes aside, the community there was quite supportive. In fact, it was at the nursing home that I took my first steps since the paralysis. They asked me if I had walked. I said I hadn't since the condition materialized. I still remember the guy going like, "Well, we're gonna put you on a walker and we're gonna make you walk." That's where I took my first steps. And before I knew it, I was in Connecticut living with my great aunt Nancy again.

Here ComeS the Money

Chapter Twenty-Four

When I moved to my aunt Nancy's again, I was residing on the second floor, and my brother had to carry me on his back to take me upstairs. That's because I could walk but not upstairs. My legs hadn't fully regained their strength. Living there for a while, I gained a sense of normalcy, but there was a level of dependence that I was no longer comfortable with.

Fortunately, money rolled in from 2005 car accident. If you recall, this is the car accident that caused me to become paralyzed. Once I had the money to move out, I did move out and away and found myself back in North Carolina. There I met a girl and was back on my emotionally-restrained relationship train. I lost a lot of the money in the process. I learned some valuable lessons by having all that cash. The first is to never buy someone a car if you can't afford to buy them ten cars. You don't know how much you need the money you have until you've spent it getting someone a car that they crash.

The second important lesson is to never invest in a venture proposed by your girlfriend's son. Chances are, your hormones are involved in the decision-making. And that's not very good for business. Finally, I learned that money would attract the appearance of everything you've wanted, but you must be smart enough to see if it's the real thing.

I had seriously considered making amends with my ex-wife, and she ended up visiting a couple of times. In the process, I saw that she was with other men and got my reality check pretty quickly. I'm glad I didn't lose more money in the process, though. I used to have my money (about $17,000) at the time, locked up with the key just around the house.

However, one day I had the strong urge to keep the key with me. I placed it in my back pocket instead of my usual front pocket, and I kept the briefcase under my bed and slept. That night, I realized my ex-wife and her boyfriend were in my room looking for the key. Fortunately, I was lying on top of it, and they couldn't get it.

But that's when I realized that the toxicity of my ex-wife was something I should permanently wash my hands with. More importantly, I was still not completely mobile, and to invite people into my house while holding that much cash was going to spell disaster. So the next day, I took the money to my pastor and gave it to him to hold.

I have learned a lot from having money and from being broke. Ultimately the value of it all comes down to the people you are around. Being broke around caring people will feel alright, while being rich around the wrong people will only make you paranoid. Pay attention to who you hang out with.

Movement and ConStantS

Chapter Twenty-Five

The contrasts in your life help you cultivate appreciation. As I mentioned in the previous chapter, it was only by being both broke and cash-rich, I could tell people apart. Aside from money, there was another significant contrast in my life: that between movement and being stationary. I was often in periods of stability with Nancy's tough shadow overlooking a disciplinary regimen that I begrudgingly followed.

Around the time the lawsuit money rolled in, I had been living with her, and soon after, I started living in hotels, and nothing could be more drastic in terms of an environmental shift. I Was in a home I had grown up in one day and the next I was on my way to live in a hotel.

I reflected on the freedom that comes with living on your own and the connection and comfort of living with someone you know genuinely cares about. I also thought about the times where I lived in a crowded house with not one person who truly cared about me.

During this period, I started to build an appreciation for aunt Nancy on levels I had never noticed before. Many people will think I always held aunt Nancy in such high regard. I sure respected her and had a lot of respect for her, but I wasn't nearly as appreciative of her as you find me now. And living alone helped me realize how much I miss her.

At the same time, her discipline was so overbearing it kept me from recognizing that I need to have self-discipline. For the longest time, I was simply relying on her rules to keep my life in order. And time and time again, I faced the problem where whenever I was left to my own devices, my life would go downhill. It was like her need to protect me had left me unable to be free of her presence and prosper.

From living in different hotels, I moved to the nursing home and then out and into my own apartment. These shifting environments made me realize how I was retaining my personality across each. This was a great leap in my self-development.

Previously, I would be more of a product of my environment, closer to drugs in Connecticut, more church-centered in Carolina, and so on. But now, it was as if the pain I carried went everywhere with me and made sure I was acting the same way. In 2009 I met

Nancy again and even found out about a sister from my dad's side that I did not even know about. I thought finding out about her was going to be the highlight of that Connecticut visit, but little did I know an earth-shattering event was about to hit my life that year.

A Period of Farewells

Chapter Twenty-Six

In the October of 2009, I received a call. I was away from Connecticut as I had moved to build a life in North Carolina. On the call, I learned that aunt Nancy had suffered an aneurysm and was in the hospital. I didn't have the finances to travel there and asked God for support. I did not want my last meeting with her to be the final one.

    I learned that her sons were going to visit her. They were coming from Georgia and would pass through my state. I thought I could hitch a ride that way, but that didn't happen. I still took slower transport channels to try my best to make it.

    I would have been in Pennsylvania or New York when I heard the Lord's voice. "I will show you a miracle," He said. And the same day, I received a call letting me know that Nancy was taken off life support. I made my peace with not getting to say goodbye to her alive, but I was at least going to pay my respects to the body.

So I persisted and reached Connecticut a few days later. And the miracle manifested itself: she had stayed alive during this time. In fact, she stayed alive without life support for five whole days. To this day, I believe that she stayed alive through sheer willpower in order to meet everyone for the last time. When she passed away on October 21st, 2009, she was in the company of people who loved, admired, and respected her.

I was reeling from this loss and getting closer to my brother in the process. We talked about our mother, and eventually, I connected with her as well. We talked over the phone and sometimes in person. 2010 was the year she accepted Jesus Christ as her personal savior, but it was also the year she got liver cancer.

We moved her to a hospice, and she insisted on being away from the hospital bed. "I don't want to die here," she would say. The medical supervisor took me to the side and told me she wasn't going to make it. He said the hospice was going to be where she was likely to pass away, and it would be more comfortable than if we took her back home.

At hospice, if she's in pain, he explained, they could give her the right meds to ease the pain. It made sense, so we left her at the hospice. I still stayed in touch over the phone. One day she called and sang me a hymn. I knew it was close. And soon after, I received news that my mother, too, had passed away.

Death LingerS

Chapter Twenty-Seven

When I heard about my mom's passing, I did not cry. I believe that was because I expected her to pass away, unlike aunt Nancy whose death came out of nowhere. Moreover, I had cried myself dry with Aunt Nancy's passing; I frankly didn't have enough tears left in me.

Since that time, I had been working on myself and recovering from the losses. 2011 was the year where life and fortune seemed to be in purgatory. I didn't experience much and got to come out of my shell thanks to a girlfriend. I was no longer focused solely on sex, and in bonding with her, the humane side of me got to re-emerge. This was happening around the tail-end of 2011. But before the story could take an upward turn, she too ended up dying on me.

I still remember her parents calling me and asking for her sister to be put on the phone. And once they talked, she returned with a solemn expression. I had lost enough loved ones to know how it goes from there onward, but some part of me didn't want it to be true. I wanted to question my way out of it.

"What is it?" I asked, hoping with every cell in my being that it wasn't the kind of news that shook my 2009 and 10. "She's passed away," I heard. The world around me went silent. After all the damage my ex-wife had done, I had finally decided to come out of my shell, and I get whipped right back.

Needless to say, I wasn't on the greatest terms with God around this period. My girlfriend, who tried her best to stay independent despite being on dialysis, was gone. And then my pastor died the same year. I remember hurrying to gather myself: I had to present a courageous front for the funeral.

When they were laying my pastor to rest, I received news that my grandma, too, had passed away. And just like that was free of my own identity. So much of my life was built around the love I received from specific people, and wanting to live up to their expectations that their passing left me hollow.

Who was I? What was I going to do? And the answer was right there: return to my mission. I had the gift of speaking in tongues; I was capable of receiving the right words at the right time. Above all, I had the sheer willpower to keep going despite being broken in many ways. This was the point in my life where I could take everything from the life I had lived thus far and turn it into pure productivity. My time to do right by my mission had finally come. And it all started with my move away from both Connecticut and North Carolina.

A FreSh Start

Chapter Twenty-Eight

Every now and then, one needs a fresh start. It helps you find yourself in a different context and think outside the box. I got my fresh start when I moved away from the two places I had been the most familiar with. I t was no longer an option to be in Connecticut or in North Carolina. I was no longer ping-ponging between these two regions.

From December of 2012 to October of 2013, I lived in a trailer. Not alone, again, I was with enough people to constitute two families. The trailer was a two-bedroom arrangement, and I lived in the living room. Not the most aesthetically pleasing arrangement, but it worked. And even though I wasn't at the financial peak of my life, I felt freer as I was towards something more meaningful.

The area I was staying in now was situated in Martinsburg, West Virginia. And the church I attended there was multicultural. I have always loved the diversity and connecting with Hispanics, African Americans, and Caucasians while sharing the same passion for Christ was a wonderful experience.

This still was a painful period, and I was healing gradually, but instead of hurting without a point, I was cultivating a strong character. Character is one of the most important traits a human can have.

As you know by now, I've been rich and broke, lived in an apartment and in the projects, been a deacon and a drug user. Through it all, you get to retain one thing: your character. Everything else comes and goes, but your character stays. That is what I appreciated about this church, and meeting the right people there helped me stick to my journey.

That's what is important about one's character. Previously I had constantly found myself thrown off the church path at the mildest inconvenience and then found my way back on track, but this time around, despite every wound on my heart fresh and aching, I carried on with my journey. I stuck around and kept pushing all the way till 2015.

In 2015, I went overseas on a mission to Panama, and we didn't live in Panama City. We lived in a remote area, and I saw how other people were living. This was a great opportunity for me to count my blessings. They didn't have running water, and a week's supply was carried up the mountains once a week. They had to use the woods to go to the bathroom. This journey was character-building, to say the least. And I am glad I went on that mission. When I returned, I was coming back to a mix of disappointment and joy.

Grief and Joy

Chapter Twenty-Nine

2016 was the year where joy began to outweigh grief. While the biggest letdown was finding out that the girl I had invested so much emotion and time in as a potential partner had no interest in me in that capacity. She saw me as more of a brother, and us wanting different things disappointed us both. But there was much more going on, on the positive side.

I got elevated to the rank of minister. This was huge for me because for the longest time; I had been on a plateau as far as my upward mobility with churches is concerned. Of course, I had myself to blame for not sticking around long enough in any specific area or with a single church. But now that I had the character and engagement to persevere, things were looking up.

2017 came around, and my brother got married. I couldn't attend the wedding, but he did bring his lady to me and got my blessing before getting married. Honestly, this meant a lot because, in Nancy's presence, it was always about us competing. I didn't feel like the elder brother growing up because I was in the wagon while he was the one cycling. But when he gave me that respect, it was as if somebody had patted that inner child in me who was hurt being the black sheep all those years.

My relationship with God improved significantly as I looked back and saw how everything connected. I had to go through countless slip ups to cultivate the patience required of me when I deal with youngsters. I wasn't going to be the minister who scares the youth away from God. I was the man who brings them closer by having infinite patience and a lot of empathy for them.

I had been in the lowest of lows and could understand where the people who need God the most dwell. I was not going to be the church leader who comfortably preaches to the choir. I had already brought the message to people who didn't even know they needed God. My mother, for once, didn't think much of the bible yet accepted Jesus Christ as her personal savior before passing away.

Not only was I a minister and an effective one at that, I eventually got accepted as an elder in training. You can see from my life's story thus far that only once I committed fully to my mission, in the service of the lord, did everything painful disappear. I now was in a state of eternal gratitude and had only one wish: to find love.

Love CompleteS Life

Chapter Thirty

I was in a place where I was content, and this was closer to 2018, but I needed one last piece. You know, as well as I do, that love completes life. Sacrificing love for other things almost always leaves one with regret. I had a history that led me to believe I was never going to settle down with anyone. I had started with an attempt to save myself for marriage, and the person I lost my virginity to, eventually became my wife but seemed to do so with the sole intention of tormenting me.

But who would have thought that during a random Facebook browsing session, I was going to find love? I was on one of our church groups on Facebook and noticed this girl with an attractive profile picture. I think to myself, "Lord, should I pursue?" And I learn that I must pursue her. If I went by my own instincts, I might have rejected myself, but I gave it a shot. I messaged, saying something along the lines of "bless you, beautiful, how are you" I received no reply.

Well, that was expected, so I just continue with my day. Later, I received a reply Renea, and we start messaging back and forth. At one point, I say, "Hey, I am not very good with messaging. I like to talk on the phone." She replies with a question, "are you saying that just to get my number?" "Girl, I might be."

From there, we exchange numbers and start talking regularly. She was in Georgia, and of course, I wasn't. In March of 2019, we met, and the experience was blissful; just the company of her was more than everything I had ever done with all the other girls combined. And mind you, I had a fair share of threesomes. I can honestly say I was in heaven. That's when I asked her to be my girl, and she agreed.

In February of that year, she got into an accident. I received the pictures of the car, and it's totaled. My heart begins thumping in my chest so hard. All the previous trauma of losing loved ones comes bubbling up, and with every fiber of my being, I'm praying, "Lord, please save her." I find out she's fine but also learn in the process that I truly love her.

Seven months later, I end up getting hit by a car, and I was not fine by any definition. I got hit right in the wheelchair and developed PTSD. But she came over and served as my aide thinking nothing of her plans and situation. That's when I found out she, too, truly loves me. And the long and short of it is that she's sitting by my side as my wife as I write these closing sentences to my life story so far.

If you have finished this book, you may have taken your own lessons from it, but one thing I want to convey is that no matter what happens, you have to keep going. If you repent a million times and sin a million and one times, repent again because you have to keep going. If you love someone and get heartbroken, you must learn to love again because you have to keep going. If you fail at a hundred things but find the hundred and first opportunity, you gotta take your shot because you have to keep going.

About The Author

Jerry Linsom Jr is a Husband, Encourager, Listener, Loves People and he walks in the gift of the Prophetic. Jerry has been called and is ordained in the Ministry, and has been doing so for 25 years. Jerry is the oldest of Four Children and member of The ATS Family.

Connect With Me

Facebook- facebook.com/jaychosen.linsom

Vybn- https://sharingourwealth.com/social/timeline&u=PJerry&ref=se

LinkedIn - Prophet J.Linsom Jr

Trient Press: https://www.trientpress.com/

Assembly of Wanderers: https://atstv.tv

www.ingramcontent.com/pod-product-compliance
Lightning Source LLC
Chambersburg PA
CBHW020249010526
44107CB00002B/163